30 Minutes
...To Write a
Business Plan

Brian Finch

KOGAN
PAGE

YOURS TO HAVE AND TO HOLD
BUT NOT TO COPY

First published in 1997
Reprinted 1997, 1998

Kogan Page Limited
120 Pentonville Road
London N1 9JN

British Library Cataloguing in Publication Data
A CIP record for this book is available from the British Library.

ISBN 0 7494 2364 1

Typeset by Florencetype Ltd, Stoodleigh, Devon
Printed in England by Clays Ltd, St Ives plc

CONTENTS

The 30 Minutes Series

The Kogan Page 30 Minutes Series has been devised to give your confidence a boost when faced with tackling a new skill or challenge for the first time.

So the next time you're thrown in at the deep end and want to bring your skills up to scratch or pep up your career prospects, turn to the *30 Minutes Series* for help!

Titles available are:

30 Minutes Before Your Job Interview

30 Minutes Before a Meeting

30 Minutes Before a Presentation

30 Minutes to Boost Your Communication Skills

30 Minutes to Succeed in Business Writing

30 Minutes to Master the Internet

30 Minutes to Make the Right Decision

30 Minutes to Prepare a Job Application

30 Minutes to Write a Business Plan

30 Minutes to Write a Marketing Plan

30 Minutes to Write a Report

30 Minutes to Write Sales Letters

Available from all good booksellers.
For further information on the series, please contact:

Kogan Page, 120 Pentonville Road, London N1 9JN
Tel: 0171 278 0433 Fax: 0171 837 6348

INTRODUCTION

The plan primarily is a communication tool, designed to transmit information to a wide range of people: financiers, prospective business partners, staff, head office, or any number of others. It is occasionally (but very rarely) used as an aid to actually decide what to do, or what strategy to pursue. The plan may, for example, aim to:

- seek approval for the next 12 months' proposed activities

- raise finance from banks and investors

- help to sell or value a business

- obtain approval from regulators or grant issuing authorities.

In each case the purpose is to elicit a desired response. The plan is therefore a selling document. That applies equally to plans for internal or external use. If an internal business plan does not influence people's behaviour, what purpose does it serve? To make it effective you must focus on what response you want and from whom and then work through how to obtain it. For instance, don't produce a fund-raising document if you are actually trying to sell the business. Never forget to tell the reader what response is wanted and ask for it because, just as with any selling process, 'closing the deal' is crucial.

Think about your audience:

- Who are they?
- What do they want in a business plan?
- What language will they understand?

If you are talking to financiers you may need to include more financial information. If you are addressing the marketing director of a potential business partner you may need to devote more time to explaining market synergies. If you are addressing your staff you need to tell them what you want them to do and fill them with enthusiasm to do it. Give the information that your audience needs. If you aren't sure who may read your plan, try to cover all the likely targets.

Think also about what will alienate your audience. Don't mislead or omit significant information, but thinking about what may upset your audience affects *how* information is presented.

Avoid jargon

Avoid using jargon, mnemonics or abbreviations that the reader will not understand. Proposals are often passed on by the original recipient – who may understand technical terms – to a general manager or a finance manager, who may not and could find the jargon confusing and off-putting.

Try to use simple English and clearly explain concepts that a layperson may not understand, especially when dealing with government departments and regulators or when the reader is not English. Check your document by asking someone who does not know your business to read it. Can they understand your proposal?

Professional assistance may help provide a detached perspective or strategic advice but the business managers should produce the first draft. This document will form the basis for subsequent presentations: if you are unfamiliar with plans you must talk about, you will not convince anyone.

You are telling a story

Before beginning to write you must have a clear idea of the story you are telling. It can help to jot down notes of the key features so as to get it all into order and produce an outline.

A story should have a beginning, a middle and an end. The beginning is the background to your organisation and activity and how you got to this point; the middle is what your business is all about; and the end is what you propose. A story grabs the attention of the reader and stimulates interest and imagination. It flows . . . so should a business plan.

As with a novel it is important to remember the plot, the descriptive bits (background or scene setting) and the characters. Your plans and background are essential but so are the people who will carry it out. Don't get the balance wrong and waffle on about the market or the history of the business. Don't bore your reader.

There is no ideal length. A small business can be complicated and require a lot of explanation, while a large business can be comparatively simple. Be as brief as you can.

Use action words

Think of your plan as an adventure story, not literary criticism: use action words as much as possible to say what you will do and when, rather than describing scenery. Some description may be called for, but remember that brevity and actions have more impact in a business plan.

You must stimulate the reader's enthusiasm for your project so that he or she will 'buy in' to it. The story of you, your business and what you propose to do with it is a fascinating story: tell it that way.

Finally, this is not a recipe book. Every organisation is different and so, therefore, is every business plan, but there are nonetheless basic minimum requirements that will need to be addressed: these are covered in the checklist in the Appendix. This is structured for a business but it works for public service organisations also.

1

THE STRUCTURE OF THE PLAN

1. Start with a summary

You probably only have a few minutes to make a good impression with your plan. By the time the reader has finished the summary and maybe the introduction you have won or lost.

Your first objective is to grab the reader's attention – not with some gimmick, but because the proposal is interesting. The summary is the way to do this. Before the reader knows it they know the outline of your case and are interested. They read on, already willing to be convinced. Conversely, if the first page creates a poor impression, it is hard to change it.

The summary should almost never be more than a page long. It should not include all the evidence for your case, just an outline of the most important points. It says what the situation is and what is proposed.

Example

This proposal is for a world-class business to be established in XXXX in partnership with YYY. It is envisaged that this would be the first of at least five facilities to be built to provide national coverage over a ten-year period. Total investment would exceed £100m, 200,000 jobs might be created, economic activity worth £500m per annum could result and government tax revenues would approach £100m per annum.

This facility will use the latest technology and processes to enhance quality and efficiency and ensure the maximum safety of employees. It will raise the possibility of significant exports to surrounding countries as well as displacing imports.

YYY is a truly international company with a proven track record of working in rapidly developing countries with local partners and has developed local skills in its new operations.

The main benefits of this proposal are:

- agricultural development
- transfer of technology
- encouragement of local manufacturing
- potential exports and import substitution
- additional economic growth, higher tax revenues and increased employment

We seek:

- a production licence for the first plant
- permission to import some key equipment for construction.

We have identified local partners who have expressed initial interest in the project.

However, the summary cannot be written until everything else in the business plan has been completed. Choose the key points from within the plan itself, decide on their relative balance and summarise them. The summary is like the synopsis on the dust-jacket of a book that persuades someone to buy it.

2. The background

As with a story, it is important to set the scene. Let the reader know the history of the organisation or business. For a new enterprise give some history of the market or service, how it has developed and where you think it is going.

- What does the organisation do?
- Where does it do it?
- How does it do it?
- Does it sell a product or service and, if so, how?
- Does it have key suppliers, customers or staff?
- How many outlets or factories does it have?
- How big is it? (turnover? profits? staff?)

For a start-up with no trading history there should be some background to the market, competitors and management team. If the background suggests operational problems explain how they arose, what has been learned and how they will be or have been resolved.

For some businesses their regulation is a key aspect of the story. Regulations may not be at the heart of operating a retail outlet but for such things as casinos, amusement machine hire, nursing homes, food distribution and road haulage they are.

The people

Say something about yourself and the rest of the people who run the organisation.

Research shows that the most important factor for investors in evaluating a proposal is the management team. This is the place to review the organisation structure and the skills of the organisation as a whole and key people within it.

If you feel that you are not a balanced team, it may be a good idea for the plan to address the issue. Perhaps you should bring someone in to provide skills you don't have, or perhaps you can propose how the weakness will be addressed at the appropriate time.

The skills that you do have should be presented well. Tell the reader about the individual responsibilities of the management team if these are not obvious. Give background information on each member of the top management team. Give their age, relevant academic or professional qualifications, experience in the industry and job they are doing or will do, highlights of past employment experience, share stake in the company (if they have one). List each person's *achievements* and emphasise career progression. Emphasise experience, qualifications and strengths that are *relevant* to their current or proposed role. For example:

John Smith BSc FCCA, Finance Director (age 41)
Joined the company as finance director in 1987, having been group financial controller with Jones Amalgamated Plc from 1985 until its takeover by Mega Corporation in 1987. He was responsible for all financial reporting at Jones, was closely involved in their £120m rights issue in 1986 and was part of the bid

> defence team. Previous experience includes two years as finance director of a £70m turnover mechanical contracting subsidiary of Stronson plc, during which time he oversaw installation of a new computer and accounting system.

For a fund-raising document it will probably be appropriate to put a more detailed CV for each key manager in an Appendix. These should only be a page long but should give some educational details and information about responsibilities and *achievements* in each previous job.

Some people are too proud to sell themselves. They give general background information but few hard facts. You can succeed despite this attitude, but why create unnecessary difficulties? The better your story, the better the impression you create.

Show your organisational structure:

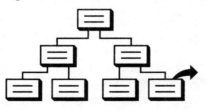

You are a team and an organisation and you must demonstrate the ability of both. Show how the organisation works and explain what is relevant. Give numbers of staff employed in particular areas to show the level of responsibility of managers.

People are uneasy about backing one-man or one-woman companies – but many businesses are driven by one powerful personality, especially in the early days. Will one or two people become overloaded? What happens if one key individual is ill? Does the whole enterprise grind to a halt? Demonstrate an effective team which can cope with the day-to-day issues on its own. For small businesses or organisations it may be impractical to have a back-up. One way of dealing with this is to take out life insurance and permanent health policies.

Financiers will often seek references from previous business colleagues on management teams they back. Have yours ready – and be sure that they will say nice things.

3. Outline of the business/organisation

Your audience may know nothing about your business and industry: or, worse, they may think they do and be utterly mistaken. You must educate the reader and get the key facts over quickly.

There are three sections to this explanation:

- What product or service you provide
- The marketplace you operate in
- The mechanics of how you provide the product or service.

The product or service

Be selective. Don't go into pages of detail, just describe what is necessary. Every business or organisation will be different so there is no way of defining what should be included. One way of getting the balance right is to get someone else to read the plan and tell you whether they understand and whether there is too much information.

Why are you different?

If your product or service is unique make that clear. Explain why it is better than competitors. Give details, not just vague generalisations. Superiority is something you should shout about – so do. In a tough world, businesses succeed because they have some competitive advantage. Maybe the management team is outstanding, the product is new and exciting or the market is growing fast. Make sure the reader doesn't have to search for reasons to back you.

Talk about your competitors. Show that you know who they are, how they are organised, what they are doing and their strengths and weaknesses. Then say why you will beat them. Address the issue of whether the competitors can catch up or copy you and how long that will take. Very few businesses have a permanent competitive advantage unless it is protected by a patent, copyright, a strong brand or by government regulation. If you have such protection, describe it here.

The mechanics

- **Supply.** Do you have unique sources of supply? Are you especially dependent upon any one supplier? Do you use subcontractors?

- **Processes.** What are your key processes? Do you use machinery? How does it compare with competitors?

- **Distribution.** How do you deliver your product? Do you use wholesalers, sell to stores, sell directly to end-users? How do you store or transport the product?

- **Premises.** Do you have factories, offices, showrooms, shops? Do you rent or own these? Is their precise location important?

What can go wrong?

People who read business plans tend to ask, 'What is my risk, what can go wrong and what would my exposure be?' Dispel concerns. Your reader does not want to back a business that can be shut down at the whim of a far-off authority or as a result of a small error. For regulated enterprises, explain clearly how it all works and how your internal control ensures you do not fall foul of the authorities.

4. The market

Many public services or charities cannot be said to operate in a 'market', with competitors and pricing issues. However, the environment within which they operate should be described, including the key regulations and external controls on quality. For businesses describe the market.

Definition

As an example, Childco is a retailer of maternity and baby products trading in a high street in South London.

Unless Childco is planning to open more shops, the relevant market is local. What really matters is whether the birth rate is growing or static in the immediate area of this shop. So define your market and then describe its key features.

Segmentation, structure, size and trends

Are you trading in a particular niche within a larger market? If so, explain this segmentation.

Is the market fragmented, with many small firms selling products with unique characteristics, or are there a few large organisations selling a 'commodity' product where consumers see no difference between different products? How is the product or service delivered to the customer or user? Describe the features of the market structure that you feel are important.

Is the market growing, static, shrinking? The reader wants to know what might happen, however speculative. By raising issues you can disarm them before they can create a negative aura around your project.

Competitors

Many plans describe businesses without competitors or dismiss them lightly. Just because a competitor makes an inferior product you will not necessarily beat them in the marketplace. They may be more astute managers or have a link with the key distributor . . .

Issues that determine competitive success include distribution, pricing, brand strength, packaging and promotion as well as financial strength. Set out these issues, briefly.

Think also about **potential** competitors. For example, a telephone company may one day become a media company or a publisher of financial information.

Explain who your **relevant** competitors are. The children's shop, in the example referred to above, competes with another independent retailer nearby, with a branch of a national chain a few hundred metres away, and also with mail order catalogues and chain stores that have children's departments. Other shopping centres are also competitors.

Are there alternative products? These are also competitors.

How do you compete?

Explain whether the market is price-sensitive, dependent upon location of outlets, driven by quality of product or service, etc.

Describe the important factors about the key competitors. The reader needs enough information to assess whether you can compete effectively.

Customers

The customer is another ingredient missing from many business plans. Who are yours? Is your customer a store or supermarket buyer? Talk about your buyer, but don't ignore the end-user who takes the product from the store's shelves. You will inspire confidence.

Do you have any dominant customers who represent a very high proportion of your sales?

5. Trading summary

For an existing trading business, summarise its past performance and its future expectations. For public services, charities and other non-profit-making organisations, there is a similar process of evaluating what has been delivered in the past and at what cost. For a housing association, for example, it may be the number of people accommodated and at what cost.

There is no right or wrong way to lay out these figures. I like to see the trading of the business set out first, followed by a balance sheet and finally a cash flow. Future projected figures should be set out in the same table as the past figures, so that a progression can be seen.

Don't put masses of detailed figures in the body of the plan – put them in an appendix and summarise them in this section.

Example: new retail business

Sometimes a more detailed breakdown of sales or expense categories will be appropriate in the summary of trading. Usually the minimum information requirement will be:

- Turnover
- Gross profit

Summary data on proposal					
£000	Year 1	Year 2	Year 3	Year 4	Year 5
Number of shops	2	4	12	20	28
Turnover	1,620	3,451	10,670	18,720	27,682
Profit before interest & tax	−95	58	482	1,092	2,040
Profit after interest and tax	−83	50	419	850	1,526
Cash flow excluding Capex	−89	59	465	1,079	2,001
Total cash flow	−409	−270	−893	−335	560
Return on net assets (Pre-int)	−28%	9%	24%	35%	49%
Square footage (year end)	6000	12,000	36,000	60,000	84,000
Sales/sq ft £	270	288	296	312	330
Stock turn	3.9	4.0	4.0	4.1	4.2

- Overheads
- Profit before interest and tax.

Assumptions

Set out the key assumptions you have made in any forecasts. These determine whether the reader believes your proposal, so give some evidence to support them. They must be correct – and you have to 'sell' them – so set them out clearly: let the reader follow your thinking without needing a computer to copy the calculation.

You will have summary forecasts in the main body of your plan, so that is where you should have the key

Example: new retail business

Key commercial assumptions

The main assumptions are that: the shops will average 2000 square feet of retail space and achieve sales (in their first year) of £310 per square foot – growing at 10 per cent per annum for the next two years. These sales densities are low by normal retailing standards. These figures are achievable through the promotional programme outlined previously.

The achieved gross margin is expected to average 35 per cent in the first year, after allowing for theft and markdowns. The margin is based upon completed negotiations with suppliers – see Appendix.

Overheads, property and staffing costs are based upon the promoters' experience of similar businesses.

assumptions. This is your opportunity to persuade readers before they have time to reach the wrong conclusions.

Make assumptions explicit. Explain important points, for example:

- Turnover fell in 1996 due to the disruption caused by relocating. This was more than made up in the following year as growth resumed

- Gross profit has improved over the years and a target of 52 per cent is usual in the industry and will be achievable now that the company is large enough to buy in bulk and get volume discounts.

Particularly in new businesses, the promoters may be relying upon the advice of outside consultants. Do some checking of major assumptions, don't just rely on others.

> *I received a business plan about a leisure business, seeking £750k. I rang several people in the industry, who were happy to discuss how it worked.*
>
> *I found out that the most important assumption in the plan, usage of the facility, was very optimistic. This damaged the credibility of the forecasts. Why on earth didn't the promoters make a couple of telephone calls to double-check their assumptions?*
>
> Corporate finance consultant

What does it mean?

The reader wants an explanation, not just data. Don't overwhelm with too many numbers.

Think: is this a good or a bad picture? Is it plausible?

Don't leave the reader to come to the wrong conclusions. Your first meeting with a potential project sponsor is not the time to be confronted with, 'I see from your forecast that . . . but this doesn't seem to be explained . . .'.

Try to show how sales and costs of sales are split by products or services you provide. If they have very different profitability, show how many units of each you propose to sell and how much profit is expected to come from each.

Most readers accept that reality has a habit of being different from all those projections. Nonetheless, if you explain your intentions convincingly, supported by numbers that describe the past and the expected future, the reader will believe that you can cope with the unexpected.

Cash, cash, cash

A business plan may show a fabulous profit projection but if you run out of cash you will never achieve it. Cash is therefore, in a sense, more important than profits.

21

Businesses never collapse because they are losing money, but because they run out of cash to pay their bills or to reinvest.

Cash is a simple idea. You can tell from your bank balance whether you can pay a bill. Profit is a more elusive idea. Of course, it is the surplus of income over expenditure over a defined period, but the timing of recognition of income and expenses, the calculation of depreciation and taxation, etc can have a significant impact. A profitable business can be haemorrhaging cash.

Growing businesses usually require cash to fund bigger stocks, higher debtors and more staff. Profits are seldom high enough to provide all of this. Even while you are making good profits you may need to raise more money. This is a critical stage for your businesses and one where they may encounter problems.

At an early stage of business development you may have heavy start-up costs or initial losses. Progress may be slower than expected.

Any business plan should include a cash flow forecast. This should be broken down into months and show detail, not just an income and an expenses line. Include some 'what-if?' scenarios in your plan. Prove that you can survive a dent to your plan. Don't try to cover every possible eventuality – just do enough to show that the enterprise is not fragile.

Don't fund opening losses with bank borrowing unless you really have no option. The setting-up costs of a business should be financed with equity capital.

Neither head offices nor bank managers like nasty surprises.

Talk about financial control in the business plan. This can only be dealt with by having an adequate accounting system for a business of your size and type. Most

> *We have come across many businesses which started without enough capital. Perhaps the bank says 'no more' just as the business starts to grow and needs cash for expansion ... Don't blame the banks, they have no duty to take risks, they are in business too; it is the entrepreneur who has used the wrong sort of funding.*
>
> Accountant

businesses that fail also have a breakdown in their financial control and information systems.

Investors also want cash out of a business.

> *Post-production businesses typically make good profits, all of which they continually reinvest in bigger and better state-of-the-art equipment. The technology is continually improving and all the competitors are buying the latest equipment. You never see any cash out of those businesses. No thanks, it's not for me.*
>
> Venture capitalist

The 'dog leg' forecast

You may feel that turnover and profits will rise dramatically as a result of your plans. Is this plausible? Look at the illustration overleaf ... Could you blame the reader for being sceptical? Recheck your assumptions and your forecasts. Get someone independent to give you some impartial advice. If you are certain go ahead, but be sure that you have convincing arguments *supported by evidence*, not just ambition: **then** try to persuade the reader.

23

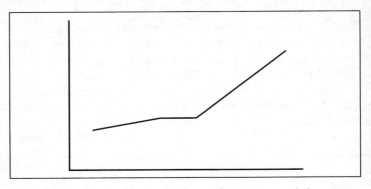

If you begin to have doubts after re-examining your evidence, don't be afraid to lower your forecasts.

On the other hand, you might be able to show how you will increase sales dramatically. You must say what those plans are and why they should succeed. Don't hide the dog leg by putting past trading in one bit of the document and the forecast elsewhere. That makes it harder to read and irritates the reader.

You may worry that the reader will knock 15 per cent off your sales forecast, whatever you put down. You may be right! The ways to combat this are

1. Give good supporting evidence for your sales forecast. The more proof, the more likely they are to believe you.

2. Show the breakeven of the business.

3. Show your fixed and variable costs (get an accountant to help you if necessary) so that a reader can quickly compute what happens if sales are, say, 15 per cent lower.

It is often useful to show a best, middle and worst case. The worst case should be truly grim and be accompanied by an explanation of how you would deal with it. Don't simply show an optimistic, a more optimistic and a very optimistic outcome.

If your proposal does not show a decent return you can:

1. Drop the project.
2. Rethink how you can do things.

What if a business plan still shows fantastic returns after reconsidering every assumption? Experience shows that things generally turn out worse than anticipated and seldom better. So put in 'contingencies' to reduce the planned profit to a believable level that is sufficient to support financing plans. *It is better to surprise with good results than to disappoint with bad results.*

6. The proposal

State your proposal clearly. *Don't forget to tell them why you are here!*

Strangely, people often devote enormous energy to writing plans but then don't ask for what they need. The plan should say very clearly what action is required from the reader. Avoid making a take-it-or-leave-it offer because you may be demanding a yes or no response where there is scope for negotiation.

A general rule is that forecasts should end at the trading profit line (after all expenses except for interest); leave the financiers to deal with the financial structure and what interest rate to apply. Leave as much as possible flexible for discussions.

Don't ask for too little. Don't pare your cost estimates to the bone and thereby underestimate your needs. It is not easy to go back and ask for more cash a few months after a government department, say, has given you a grant. On the other hand, don't ask for much more than you need;

this harms your credibility. Allow a sufficient contingency for the business going better than expected as well as worse: expansion costs money too.

Reiterate your requirements in the summary at the beginning of your business plan. Make sure the reader has not turned the first page before knowing what you want.

How much are you investing?

There are many ways to show commitment but none is as persuasive as money. If an individual is promoting an exciting business but is not prepared to invest in it, then that raises doubts. How much are the promoters investing? If it is an investment of time, then justify a value for that time. A similar issue arises with internal plans: what contribution, in terms of effort and money, is the divisional team making?

Why does the reader think like this? Your commitment convinces them that you will stick with it if the going gets tough and devote your total energy to protecting both of your investments. It has to be hard for you to walk away.

The money to be invested by the shareholders doesn't show commitment . . . while they appear to be putting in £300,000 in a £1,500,000 project they all own companies that will do work for the new business and they are charging fees that will recover their money within a year . . . so they aren't really putting in anything and we're taking all the risk!

Leasing company executive

Show salaries and fees clearly: justify them if necessary. People often seek unreasonable rewards through excessive salaries or free shares. Take professional advice on what is achievable. Be realistic.

State if funds have already been raised towards the total requirement. *If it is left unsaid in the document the financier may never pick up the phone and give you the opportunity to say it.* If money is raised after the document is written, rewrite it or add a covering letter.

How big and how fast?

You face a dilemma when you choose how big to start a business or project and how fast it should grow, because it is often more difficult to get funding for a small project than for a big one:

- Within a large group a small new project may simply not be worth the trouble
- It will be more difficult to get money out of a smaller business through its sale
- It is as much work to complete and then monitor a small deal as a large one
- To meet an investment target it may be preferable to do three big deals rather than 15 small ones
- A bigger business can afford more management and more financial control and therefore provide more information for an investor.

Investors want a high rate of return to compensate for investments that don't pay off. To achieve this an annual rate of return is set at around 30 to 40 per cent and the investor needs a business to grow fast and then to be sold within five to seven years.

How do you deal with these pressures?

If your proposal is small don't try to create a bigger business just to accommodate a financier or a head office.

27

It won't be convincing. What are your alternatives? You may be able to get funding from relatives, friends, private investors, business contacts (customers or suppliers), factoring or bank finance. Consider whether remortgaging your house or raising money on endowment policies or on your pension scheme are options you wish to pursue. Before pursuing these routes think carefully about the risks and take professional advice. Remember that if your business fails you could lose your house and your pension too.

If you are starting small but have a *clear plan for growth* then *put this in your plan*. Put forward an exciting growth strategy. Remember, though, that this should not just be a vague wish list; provide evidence to convince the reader that you are serious and will succeed. Give numbers, show you have management resources and that the opportunity really exists. Unsupported and unrealistic expansion schemes are a real turn-off!

Rapid growth places enormous strain on management to put control systems in place. It is no accident that many of the fastest growing companies collapse. If you plan rapid growth explain clearly how you will control it.

> The accounts department can't send out all the invoices as quickly as usual so customers don't pay. The computer can't cope with the number of entries going through and keeps on 'crashing'. Staff are busy on other things so management accounts aren't produced regularly. The owners are busy dealing with customers so someone in the warehouse takes advantage of the lack of supervision and starts stealing stock. There is no time to train staff so they need extra supervision. Debtors are stretching, margins are falling, nobody knows what is going on . . . and sales keep growing . . . panic reigns.

7. Risks

Help the reader by telling them what might go wrong *but
also what you will do about it*. A sensitivity analysis is just
a projection of what happens if . . . Typically it is based on
sales not being as high as expected but it can also look at
costs being higher or both of these problems occurring at
once. It is usually best to start with an estimate of what
fall in sales brings the project to break even.

Why flaunt the warts on the proposal in this way?
Because the reader will look for them and your credibility
will suffer if you have not anticipated this. Presenting the
information yourself prevents the reader getting the answer
wrong (to your disadvantage). You also have an opportunity to say why the eventuality is unlikely and how you
would deal with the situation if it arose.

Often costs that appear fixed can be cut if necessary. If
trading is disastrous staff can be laid off. Marketing costs
that are essential for building a business can be cut if sales
take too long to respond. Growth may be sacrificed, but
survival may be ensured.

An example of business risks from a plan is given below.
Note that:

■ Each risk is evaluated

■ The response to things going wrong is given.

Example: new retail business

Risk factors and sensitivities
The assumptions underlying these forecasts are based
on the promoters' experience and are considered by
them to be prudent.

1. Sales

In common with all retail businesses, any shortfall has an immediate cash impact. However, the buying policy described above would allow purchases to be reduced rapidly in response and would limit the impact on cash. A 10 per cent reduction in sales throughout the forecast period would reduce the return as follows:

Year	1	2	3	4	5
Adjusted return on net assets	–40%	–10%	0%	10%	20%
Peak debt requirement (£000)	nil	480	500	1,500	2,000

This debt would be unacceptable and the response would be to slow the roll-out of new shops and to cut back central costs.

2. Profit margin

1 per cent reduction in gross profit reduces the return on net assets by 5 per cent.

Year	1	2	3	4	5
Adjusted return on net assets	–30%	5%	20%	30%	40%
Increase in overdraft required (£000)	–	50	70	200	300

3. Rent

Higher rental costs would directly affect pre-tax profits. Therefore sites must have occupancy costs of no more than 20 per cent of forecast sales.

4. Capital costs

If the fitting-out costs were £80 rather than £70 per square foot, the maximum cash requirement in year 4 would increase by around £500k. As well as an immediate cash effect, profitability is hit through the depreciation charge. The shops would have to be redesigned.

5. General risk factors
New sites may prove less successful than planned but the risk is spread over many units.

If results are weaker than anticipated, expansion can be slowed further and central costs could be reduced accordingly.

8. Public documents

Danger: prospectuses and investment advertisements

If you write a business plan that not only describes the business but invites the reader to invest, *take care!*

To protect the public from fraudulent or misleading invitations to invest, the law in many countries sets down safeguards. In the United Kingdom this is primarily governed by the Public Offers of Securities Regulations (1995) (the POS Regulations) although various Finance Acts and the Misrepresentation Act also play a part. If you invite investment from more than about 50 people, other than family and personal acquaintances, then your document is likely to be a prospectus.

Why does this matter?

1. The requirements for a prospectus include items which will cost the issuer money, eg an accountant's report.

2. The POS Regulations detail the subjects that should be covered in the prospectus. Compliance may involve far more effort than you had anticipated.

3. There is a general requirement not to issue a misleading document. In a business plan you can warn a potential investor that they must make their own enquiries to confirm key points, but if a prospectus proves misleading, an investor who loses money can sue you personally to make it good. Issuing a prospectus in the UK that does not comply with the law is also a criminal offence and carries penalties of up to two years' imprisonment.

Since a misleading statement can have such serious consequences you will want to check your plan very carefully to ensure that each phrase and claim can be justified. You will probably need help from lawyers (more expense) and the document will become increasingly dull as you cut out those phrases which are true but hard to prove.

What is an investment advertisement?

If a document is sent to people in the UK asking them to invest in a scheme, it is an 'investment advertisement'.

An investment advertisement – regardless of whether it is also a prospectus – is regulated by the Financial Services Act 1986. This demands that the advertisement is approved by an authorised person (ie an accountant or solicitor – yet more expense). Again, if you ignore this precaution there is a danger of being sued if things go wrong.

What should you do to avoid expense and risk?

1. Banks and financial institutions are exempt bodies and are expected not to need protection – other than from

falsehood – none of the following need apply to them. However, if you send documents to accountants or financial intermediaries who may pass them on (because you haven't asked them not to) then you must assume your document is a prospectus.

2. Number each document and send out no more than 50. Instruct the recipient (in the document) not to pass it on to anyone.

3. Make clear on the front cover that the document is a business plan or information memorandum and not an invitation to invest. Say that the potential investor should take professional advice, is expected to make further enquiries and that the document is only intended to arouse interest to pursue the matter further.

4. Don't set out a clear scheme with so many shares available at so much per share. Don't include a subscription form.

Of course, accuracy should be a priority for anyone who produces a business plan, even if it isn't a prospectus. You may still be at risk from legal action. If you are sending documents overseas you must abide by the laws of the country you are sending them to, and should seek professional advice.

Due diligence – cutting the cost

If a business plan is either an investment advertisement or a prospectus extra obligations to the recipient are incurred. The most important of these is that the people issuing the document must take responsibility for it after making 'due and careful enquiry' – a process called due diligence or verification.

It is usual to employ accountants and lawyers to help. The document is reviewed line by line and all statements, claims, descriptions and observations are checked to ensure there is supporting evidence for them.

If there is any risk that a plan may require verification keep a file of supporting documentation. This may include:

- Tables of statistics

- Expert or government reports

- Internal documents

- Extracts from newspapers, magazines and trade journals

- Competitors' brochures and published reports and accounts.

All the directors of a company must sign a 'responsibility letter' acknowledging their responsibility for the document, even if they have not themselves produced it. This focuses minds on the possible consequences of a misstatement. The lawyers will write a letter of 'advice' to the directors. To avoid delay and cost it is prudent to prepare in advance for verification.

There will often be some uncertainty about points in a prospectus. You may decide to take some risk, recognising that if something goes wrong and someone decides to sue, you may have a personal liability. You must judge the commercial risk. Good luck.

THE INTERNAL BUSINESS PLAN

It is a common misconception that a formal business planning process provides managers and business planners with a strategic plan. In practice, this is rarely the case, for strategy is not the consequence of planning but the opposite: its starting point. The written plan is about implementing strategy, not forming it: 'Planning helps to translate intended strategies into realised ones, by taking the first step that can lead to effective implementation.'*

This does not make the preparation of an internal plan a less valuable exercise. On the contrary, it helps to focus minds on the most appropriate ways of achieving the desired goals. Equally, the communication of the plan and the discussion it generates usually help to generate new ideas, improve the decision-making process and direct energies and talents in the same direction.

---

* Henry Mintzberg, *The Rise and Fall of Strategic Planning.*

For these reasons a business plan forms the cornerstone of the Investors in People standard. Investors in People is a nationally recognised standard of excellence in the UK. It acts as a framework for improving business performance and achieving business goals through the utilisation, training and development of people. It has been designed by employers for organisations seeking continuous improvement.

9. What is different about internal plans?

The business plan produced for internal purposes generally serves different purposes from the external plan; hence the differences in the way they are written. The main purposes of an internal plan are:

- Communication
- Coordination and control
- Performance management.

On occasions the plan will be produced to persuade a head office to invest in a business or project and then it is like an 'external plan' used to raise money from financiers.

If it is to be truly useful the internal business plan must focus on:

- Setting *objectives* (for the organisation and its constituent parts)
- Specifying *actions* (taken by whom and when)
- Providing a *vision* to motivate and to guide decision making
- Identifying the *training and development* required to help achieve these objectives.

36

The plan will usually analyse intended strategies and translate them into actions. The effective plan is about *ideas* and their *implementation* and should not be overwhelmed by a concentration on numbers. On the other hand, it should not just be descriptive: it should have financial information to describe and support it.

Traditionally, plans have drawn heavily on financial modelling. Such a plan suffers several drawbacks:

- It is written in the language of accountants and may be hard for non-accountants to understand or identify with
- It relies mainly on hard data when the 'soft', subjective, descriptive information about a business may be the most crucial to its success
- It is often inflexible. Within weeks of its production, events in the 'real world' may make it redundant
- If it is a large and detailed document, there is a danger of it being put on a shelf, never to be referred to again.

10. How to use plans to help run businesses

Let us consider the three important ways (referred to above) in which a business plan may help to run a business:

Communication

Communication is the most important function of any business plan:

- It provides a focus for the top team to discuss issues, make decisions, share ideas and address conflicts
- As people contribute to the development of the plan, a sense of ownership is created, which assists implementation, as well as improving communication of problems and issues

- The final plan should be disseminated throughout an organisation so that it helps managers and staff alike to see the whole context of their organisation, which:

  — helps to develop pride in *their* business and *their* contribution to its success;

  — assists people to make more appropriate day-to-day decisions that further the organisation's strategy;

  — promotes openness and trust and helps morale;

  — results in ideas being generated at all levels in the organisation.

These effects can make a dramatic difference to the effectiveness of an organisation and the profitability of a business.

Confidentiality

Some people are concerned about writing down and circulating top secret strategies which might be leaked to competitors by disloyal staff. This is seldom a realistic fear. You can omit sensitive information, but how can you manage your staff without telling them what they are to do?

It is often helpful to produce a synopsis to disseminate rather than a complete plan. This helps both to convey the relevant information in a readable form and to avoid breaches of confidentiality. Detailed financial analysis can often be left out of such a synopsis.

Coordination and control

Establishing objectives for an organisation overall leads on to setting objectives for the departments and activities within it. The business plan coordinates the different parts of the organisation to work together towards its goals.

New projects, new investment proposals, etc are subsequently judged according to whether they support the attainment of the planned objectives.

The business planning process will often establish priorities, which encourages effective action.

Performance management

By establishing individual goals and work plans, a business plan can be the starting point of a performance management programme.

The plan can be used to measure individual, departmental or business performance against the objectives and milestones that have been established. The comparison can be used to refine or redefine objectives and timing and to take action to bring progress back on track.

The performance of individuals and particular parts of the organisation can be judged against the targets set in the plan itself or agreed subsequently in order to achieve it. This may affect remuneration, investment, etc.

11. Why business plans often don't work

The biggest problem arises from trying to use the planning process to formulate strategy. Although there are many books that explain how to analyse strategic issues and options, none satisfactorily explains exactly *how* to turn this analysis into a strategy. Henry Mintzberg in *The Rise and Fall of Strategic Planning* suggests that this is because producing strategy is an exercise in intuition and inductive reasoning which is at odds with the analytical and deductive reasoning that is used in the planning process. Planning, he argues, shuts off and excludes possibilities – it does not explore and develop them.

12. Setting objectives

An internal business plan details actions to be taken to meet objectives. It must therefore define those objectives. In turn they must:

- Be rational and meaningful
- Be clear and unambiguous
- Be achievable
- Be consistent
- Have a target date for completion; and
- It must be possible to measure whether they have been attained.

This last condition may be difficult in the case of 'soft' objectives, such as customer perceptions. In such cases customer or staff surveys may be useful. However, I am not a believer in objectives that are so soft they are practically liquid.

I was once involved in a planning process where the divisional head proposed such objectives as 'to be recognised as the market leader'. The division was around half the size of the actual market leader, which showed no signs of faltering. The plan did not put forward any ideas to close the gap – so it failed the first three tests listed above.

There is no simple division between objectives and strategies – they come in tiers. For example, in order to achieve 10 per cent sales growth, we must achieve a 5 per cent growth in market share so the growth in market share becomes a secondary objective as well as part of the strategy. In order to increase market share there may be other objectives to meet, such as 10 per cent increase in the sales force.

Ineffective plans are full of unconnected statements. Effective plans show how one objective (or strategy) leads to the attainment of the next.

13. The corporate vision:
soft data and hard data

We all have a touching faith in 'hard data', despite the fact that experience shows it is very often wrong. For example, market surveys are often presented as precise numbers even though they may be based on rough-and-ready estimates. When you forecast next year's growth to be 4.75 per cent the one thing you can be certain of is that it will not be exactly that.

Once one accepts that 'hard data' is itself uncertain, the descriptive elements of the plan assume greater importance.

One example of the use of 'soft data' in organisations are mission statements. At best these encapsulate a vision of where the organisation aspires to go, what it is trying to do, how goals will be achieved and why the company differs from its competitors. At worst, these mission statements are meaningless drivel.

What is essential is the vision that they express. Is it valid and does the written statement help staff to achieve it? Managers frequently hold a vision in their heads rather than having it written down. It provides inspiration, encapsulating something unique about the business that will guide decisions and actions. It can be an enormously powerful motivator to management and staff who understand and share the vision and are enthused by it.

The 'information' that makes up the vision for a business is not analytical, numerical or 'hard data' but soft data, which comprises the views, opinions and perceptions of the people who work in the business and of customers and suppliers, encompassing intuition about the way markets, customers and suppliers will behave in the future. Soft data is arguably more reliable than hard data and a business plan should certainly contain it. Many studies show that the best strategic management decisions are made intuitively, even though detailed analysis may have *informed* the judgement.

14. Involving staff: building the team

Whether the purpose of the plan is to guide management action or to raise money, it needs:

1. Ownership by all of those who are required to carry it out

If people don't believe in a plan they will not make it happen. At best they will acquiesce but without enthusiasm; at worst they will sabotage it. They won't believe in a plan:

- that is imposed from above
- if they are not consulted in its formation
- if they disagree with targets and proposed actions to meet them.

But ownership will lead to . . .

2. Commitment

Wanting to succeed leads to enthusiasm and:

- hard work — achieving the unachievable
- feedback — when management gains valuable business information
- ideas — that assist the achievement of the plan
- customer service — committed staff deliver better customer service
- communication — with superiors, subordinates, customers and suppliers improves with commitment.

42

Budgets which managers think are unachievable invariably damage morale. However, *involvement* in preparing the plan, even if it is only their part, understanding the overall plan and believing in it helps people to find ways to achieve difficult targets.

15. Successful communication

Information must be relevant to the audience. Avoid staff leaving a meeting thinking 'so what?'

Ideally, staff should be told about plans for the business by their line managers. The plans should – where possible – not be presented as a *fait accompli*. People should feel involved in developing the plans for their particular 'area' to meet the overall corporate plan.

Most business plans are about change – this explains some of the resistance to communicating them, since managers fear staff resistance to change. However, where staff could feel threatened by possible loss of status or even jobs, effective communication is more not less relevant. Be open; discuss problems if possible. If the threat is real then those affected should be told the whole story at once; uncertainty is not only unpleasant but also harms performance (fear and uncertainty are poor motivators).

Time and thought should therefore be given to how the plan is to be communicated effectively. Don't delay – rumour damages morale.

16. Planning for people and skills

Many business plans emphasise the importance of their staff but then ignore the skills, training and development they need to carry out that plan.

Once people are aware of the demands placed upon them by a business plan they should be involved in discussing their own training needs, to ensure they have the skills to meet the objectives.

In the UK the prime objective of the Investors in People programme is to develop and train staff to meet the objectives of the business. The identification of training needs should, in any case, be a part of an annual appraisal process.

17. Producing and using the internal plan

The following points may be particularly helpful for internal business plans:

1. Before starting, does the planning team agree who the document is for and what purposes it serves?

2. The plan does not need to be a literary masterpiece, but it must be clear and easy to read.

3. Don't confuse the business plan with the budget. The plan is about ideas, implementing them and motivating people: a budget is used to control an organisation during implementation. Ideally, a business plan should not be done at the same time as the budget or it will simply become a continuation of the budget.

4. The targets and broad thrust of the plan should be agreed at the most senior level. Then individuals and teams throughout the organisation should be involved in agreeing on actions they must take to implement it.

5. Once the plan has been developed, it should be dated and communicated straight away. Organisations and individuals move on and change fast: don't get too concerned about fine tuning. It is a *starting point* for getting *new* and *more* things done.

6. Key business objectives should be taken out of the plan and translated into short-term action plans.

7. Training and development plans should be drawn up from these key business objectives.

8. Options, or what-ifs, should be considered but can only cover a few scenarios in outline or the plan would take years to produce. A flexible plan should concentrate on setting objectives and outlining broad strategies for getting there. Detail quickly becomes outdated; objectives age more slowly.

9. Use consultants when individuals and organisations are not practised in the art of producing plans. But remember, outsiders should *facilitate* the plan, not write it. If other people write the plan the implementors are not committed to making it work.

18. Managing the process

Using senior management

The presence of senior management in departmental planning sessions can be inhibiting. Ideas may be stifled through nervousness or fear of looking stupid. Alternatively, staff may take the opportunity to question or attack company strategy or individuals within the organisation. This delays and inhibits successful planning.

Meetings need to be carefully planned. What are the objectives, who is to run them, what could go wrong? You are investing time and effort in this process – don't waste it. A skilled 'facilitator' may sometimes be needed.

Combining divisional or departmental plans

Departments, subsidiaries or divisions are often asked to contribute their plans to an overall plan. Satisfactory guidance must be given to ensure the results are useful.

Example: multinational company

The executive board of a UK company asked for business plans from its six regions and from its five head office departments. While some guidance was given to each, the responses were disappointing and did not address crucial strategic questions. Those involved were very capable people, so why did this happen?

Busy operational managers who probably had clear strategies and knew their markets very well were not used to ordering this knowledge and writing it down as a business plan. An outside consultant was involved but because of internal sensitivities was not allowed to ask questions and challenge proposals.

The lesson is that even within sophisticated organisations people who are unused to writing business plans need detailed instructions or help from someone independent to identify what is missing and prompt people to fill in the gaps.

Who is responsible for what and when?

Since a business plan should identify actions to be taken, someone must take responsibility for completing them by a given date.

In the executive meeting the operations director was given an instruction and responded, 'Yes, John.'

The simple word 'Yes' can have several meanings. It can mean; 'Yes, that's a great idea, I am totally committed and I will go and make that happen' or 'Yes, I don't like it but I'll make a show of doing it and then

> blame you when it doesn't work.' In this case it meant
> 'Yes, I hear you, I'll go through the motions but there's
> no chance of meeting such a ridiculous target.'

Make sure people really have accepted responsibility and
are committed to the objectives.

Follow-up and review

Having made commitments it is necessary to measure
progress against them. Let everyone know when progress
will be reviewed. During the review let any who have not
met their commitments explain why. Maybe reset their
objectives. If the plan itself has proved unrealistic then this
is the time to rethink – possibly the whole strategy.

If there are important 'milestones' in the plan progress
should be formally reviewed when they should have been
achieved, whenever that is. In any case, the progress of the
plan should be reviewed annually.

Some managers complain that they are constantly in
planning meetings. In a way this misses the point. If you
try to define management and planning, it is hard to come
up with significant differences. The problem lies not with
planning itself but with how it is organised – try to go into
less intricate detail, for example.

3

THE MECHANICS OF WRITING THE PLAN

19. Getting ideas together

For most people, it is difficult to get ideas into an order that can be clearly communicated. The outline in the Appendix provides a good starting point for the issues to be covered and in what order. It is not exhaustive but most people will see what is missing – for their particular business – as they go through.

If you follow this model, the next step is to put the issues into their categories. One way of doing that is to write the headings in black and the issues in red. Through matching the two lists new entries will come to mind. It is often useful for an accountant or another adviser to help by asking questions. In the UK there are schemes accessible through the Business Link organisations that may be able to provide such consultancy help at greatly subsidised prices.

For larger businesses there are two common techniques. One is to get each head of department to write a plan for their part of the business. A senior manager works with the authors to pull the plans together and get it to a final state. The objectives, strategies and constraints of the overall business may emerge from this process or they may be imposed on it. If it is the latter then the departmental plans will have to be adjusted to conform. At some stage there will have to be at least one meeting to consider all the individual plans in the context of the overall plan. The other approach is to get the coordinator to go out to the departments or divisions and write a business plan based on extensive discussion. The weakness of this is that individual managers may not feel a sense of ownership of and commitment to the plans.

Another way to get the planning process going is to gather the planning team in a room and lay out a series of postcards with subjects such as Staff/Strategy/Customers/The market/Competitors, etc written on them. Give everyone a handful of blank cards and get them to write brief thoughts about any of these and put them under the appropriate heading so that everyone can see them.

Split the resulting cards into 'actions' that managers can take and 'descriptions' of the business or its environment. Form a story line from the action cards and see how they relate to the descriptions.

This technique encourages discussion and exchange of ideas and demonstrates to the team a shared idea of the business. The initial part of the process should avoid any criticism of ideas, however ridiculous they may seem. Criticism stifles good ideas as well as bad ones. There must be no criticism of individuals, which can create enduring ill feeling and stifle ideas. Later on ideas can be rejected through discussion within the group.

20. Make it easy

You have sent your plan to a planning director or an immediate superior. This plan is the most important thing in your life at present. *Remember that it is not the most important thing in their lives!* They may have received four plans today and have a lunch meeting and two further meetings booked for the afternoon. This morning there is a list of 12 telephone calls to make and . . . How much time do you think your plan has to make an impression? You are right . . . *not long.*

- Your one-page summary has captured the reader's attention. Capitalise on your advantage
- If the plan is more than three or four pages long, put in an index
- Number the pages and maybe the points as well
- Don't waffle. If someone has to search for what matters you will turn them off
- Set out the document so that it is easy to read: put in headings; put detail in appendices; use a clear typeface, not a tiny print that the reader has to strain to read; space paragraphs out
- Date the document to avoid confusion with earlier or later drafts.
- Some people like to number each paragraph for easy reference. Some like to have a hierarchy of headings, eg:

    MAIN HEADING

    Sub-heading

    Sub-sub-heading

- Show diagrams or photographs of important products, premises, processes, etc; they will bring the subject alive for the reader

- Don't spend ages producing a computer forecast which second-guesses someone's financial structure. You have probably got it wrong. Stop at the trading result.

People do not take in long numbers when they read a document. Why then do we put masses of confusing numbers in documents where we are trying to communicate ideas? Why then do we produce tables of numbers that are hard to take in and even harder to remember? We have forgotten that we are trying to *communicate*. Accountants sometimes think that they are showing respect for accuracy if they are precise and the computer may throw out information that way. If so:

1. Get the computer to print out in a different way.
2. Put the computer print-out in an appendix and print summarised numbers in the report.
3. Who is writing this business plan, you or a computer?

For example:

Not . . .

£	1990	1991	1992
Turnover	3249612	4755816	4873245
Gross profit	837146	947888	857930
Overheads	666987	734579	789002
Net profit	170159	213309	68928

with no explanation.

Instead . . .

£000	1990	1991	1992
Turnover	3300	4800	4900
Gross profit	840	950	860
	(26%)	(20%)	(18%)
Overheads	670	730	790
	(21%)	(15%)	(16%)
Net profit	170	210	70

(a) Turnover increased by 46% in 1991 as a result of our price cutting but by only 2% in 1992 when our competitors responded.
(b) Gross profit declined from 26% to 18% over the period due to the lower prices.
(c) Meanwhile we cut overheads in relative terms from 21% to 16% of turnover.

While our strategy worked very well in the first year (profits up 24%), lack of growth in year 2, continuing fall in margin and slight increase in overheads led to a collapse in profits. We expect that this will be just as dramatically recovered, following the recent bankruptcy of our main competitor.

Ensure the numbers line up and are separated by commas. Make it clear what units are being used. Don't use physical quantities in one place and values in another – be consistent.

Where possible, communicate through graphs and diagrams rather than tables; they often tell a story more effectively; for example:

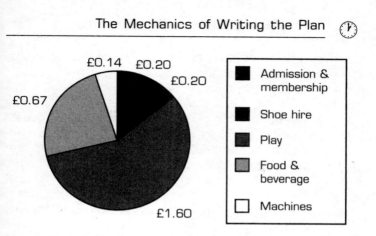

Figure 20.1: *Typical customer spend in £ per game*

However, don't get carried away and flood your business plan with unnecessary pictures. Always ask, 'What is the most effective way of communicating this idea?'

Finally, having communicated the business concept and background, don't spoil it by formulating some complicated financial scheme and don't worry about how much is due to which, why and when!

Observe two cardinal rules:

- Keep it simple
- Leave room for negotiation.

Nobody backs schemes they don't understand. Outline what you hope to achieve but don't set rigid or complex solutions. A deal gets harder to do as it gets more complex.

21. Facts → Numbers → Evidence

Your reader looks for evidence that what you are saying is true. This should be provided by putting verifiable facts in the text wherever possible. These facts should be supported by numbers to set in context how relevant the fact is and to support the projections later in the report.

It is a famous dictum of propaganda that a lie, if repeated frequently enough, becomes accepted as the truth. It seldom works in business plans. Constant repetition focuses the reader's attention on the issue and may simply reinforce a climate of disbelief. *Give the facts to support your claims: don't simply repeat the claims.*

Don't waffle! Some reports go on at great length. Even if beautifully written, it is not written for the right audience. Rather, it is being written for the writer, who is passionate about the business and very interested in him or herself. The attention of the reader is lost at the outset.

Most readers will seek confirmation of sales forecasts, either from past trading or by speaking to prospective customers. Be ready for this and provide as much supporting information as possible; market research data, published information, extracts from management accounts, customer lists, etc.

22. Cash now

One of the most important things about cash is timing – when it will turn up to fund the enterprise, when it will be needed to pay bills and when trading activities will produce it. A business can run into severe difficulties if cash is delayed, even if it is definitely on its way.

Sales   When will you receive payment from the people you sell goods and services to? If you factor debts or discount invoices, how soon will you be paid by the finance company and what proportion of the debt will they cover?

VAT   Don't forget value added tax. When will it need to be paid? For a new business you may make a large claim for VAT on pre-opening expenses. But if the registration deadline is missed the refund may be delayed.

Property taxes   Rates in the UK must be paid before you appeal against an excessive assessment. While trying to get your own money back you must cover the cost – hardship is not an acceptable excuse. When must you pay rates, insurance or property service charges? Are water rates included?

Trade suppliers   What credit terms will trade suppliers grant you? Are you sure? They may treat a smaller company differently from a large one. Cheques may not clear from your account until a week after the date shown in your forecast – giving an extra week of takings to cover it.

Professional advisers   Will professional advisers require some part of their fees paid in advance?

Taxes   It is a sad fact that many businesses pay taxes on staff wages and salaries somewhat later than they are meant to, even though this may mean an inspection and possible penalties.

23. The five-year forecast

Five-year forecasts are very useful. They are useful for scrap paper, for making paper darts and for rolling into little balls to throw into the bin on dull days.

A forecast is always useful to show the direction the organisation is heading in and what the outcome will be if everything goes according to plan. But the figures for five years time cannot be more than approximately right.

Show a summary of the forecasts for one to three years. Give a five-year forecast only if there is a good reason, such as a plan to float the company in five years, or to demonstrate how debt could be repaid in five years. It is better to show a convincing, and impressive, two or three-year outlook than a mass of numbers that nobody believes.

Always put the summary of past trading together with the forecast. *Don't* make the reader search through the document to compare past and future. *Don't* put the past and future in different formats, even if things change: the reader immediately wonders what you are hiding by making it hard to compare. For example:

£000	Year	Actual		Forecast	
		1	2	3	4
Sales					
	Product 1	100	120	130	130
	Product 2	0	0	20	30
		100	120	150	160
Gross profit					
	Product 1	20	20	25	30
	Product 2	0	0	5	10
		20	20	30	40

Put detailed figures in appendices. Nobody believes detailed expense analyses forecast five years ahead. If someone really wants such information, it can be produced on request. If key ratios (such as overheads:sales) vary significantly from one year to another, explain why.

Treat the forecast as a tool for showing broadly what will happen and why. Explain why the numbers turn out the way they do; don't force the reader to plough through detail. If there is a message, spell it out. The forecast is just the evidence for the message.

24. Why you shouldn't lie

Most people make mistakes. Management know things about their businesses that may not find favour with superiors or business partners. It is not our duty in preparing a business plan to advertise the warts on a situation, *as long as we do not dishonestly hide them.*

We must portray ourselves and our companies in the best possible light. We can be creative when we describe things by exaggerating our part in a triumph, omitting to mention a failure that can decently be ignored, using language to build an impression of excellence. That is all part of the game as long as it is not misrepresentation.

People sometimes delay the moment of reckoning. They may forget to mention the outstanding litigation, hoping that by the time the truth emerges the other party will be too committed to withdraw. It is always worth considering that obvious attempts to mislead strike at **trust**. If our business partner or superior stops trusting us, the likelihood of a *successful* deal diminishes.

Where is the line between being dishonest and 'let the buyer beware'? Most people know which side of the line they are walking – keep to the right side.

It is hard to run a company when superiors or financiers are always seeking confirmation of all information. Do not assume that an investor or a head office will stick with a deal with someone they don't trust. They may feel it is cheaper not to throw good money after bad.

I sacrificed £75,000 of legal and accountancy costs we had incurred by pulling out of a deal at the last minute when I discovered that I didn't trust the MD I was backing. The chap had held back about previous businesses he had been involved with. I don't think

> *there was anything wrong but I felt uncomfortable that he had withheld the information. Better to lose some money now than the whole investment later.*
>
> Venture capitalist

25. Don't sell your story by the kilogramme, use appendices

Tell your story with key points and summary evidence and put essential supporting data in appendices. You may want these in a separate document so that the plan does not appear too daunting. Supporting evidence may include:

cvs of the key managers

detailed forecasts

press cuttings

brochures

market survey data

map of site locations

reports by industry experts

sales data by customer, eg *key customer analysis*

product costing data

property valuations and details of leases

details of patents and technical specifications

audited accounts

Only include relevant, helpful and usable information: don't make your reader plough through unnecessary paper.

26. Timing: don't leave it so late!

The first (and only) Law of Timing

Everything always takes longer than you expect.

> *You need someone to do something urgently but they are out; then they are busy. They have other clients. They can't find the file; then they respond but it misses the post. The post takes two days instead of one. You are out on the day it arrives. You reply at once but need further information, losing a day, then your typist is sick so a day is lost; then the franking machine seizes up at 5.00 and you lose another day – and so on.*

No sensible investor will be rushed into putting money into a venture without the opportunity to investigate it properly and to think about it. Even if your proposal is extremely attractive and easy to investigate it will take *at least* four weeks to get cash from the date of the first meeting. Eight weeks is a more realistic assessment. Many private investors claim that they make decisions more quickly than financial institutions. Unfortunately, this is not my experience.

Many businesses or projects set up to prove an idea *before* seeking finance and must then find it against the background of a ticking clock. You are committed. You are losing money with every day of delay; you may miss the annual season. The investor is suspicious: 'We are being rushed, what are they trying to hide?'

Start arranging finance in plenty of time. Most people who are in a hurry could have started looking months earlier. If you are desperate you are in a very weak negotiating position.

27. Presentation is not all

Presentation is not all – but it does matter. If a document is badly typed and looks a mess, it does not inspire confidence. Poor presentation is one of the quickest routes to the waste bin.

A short, handwritten, faxed note *may* win approval – but not often. To maximise your chances, present an impressive document.

Always be prepared to invest that little extra effort to achieve perfection. It might just make the difference.

Check figures *thoroughly* before the document goes to anyone – mistakes can creep in. When the plan has been changed a hundred times and you are fed up with the thing it is easy to think that the last change won't affect anything else, but you could be wrong. That last change will not match something else in the document or it will introduce an unforeseen error in the figures. The complex sums in computer models can easily be thrown out by a small change. The error either invalidates forecasts or makes you look like a fool. Either way it undermines you and your plan. So, check everything one last time.

The document should be on good quality paper, using a good quality printer, with a title page, and should be stapled or bound. If appendices are included use page separators. Make sure that photocopies are good ones. Spend some money.

Some people mistakenly think that a beautiful document will get the necessary backing even if the plan is inadequate. A reasonable appearance is only one necessary stage to getting it read; once read, the plan must make sense. If key questions are unanswered or if there are errors, you reduce your chances. The reader may even suspect that you are trying to deceive them.

28. You only get one chance

If you tell your story clearly and include supporting data you should answer all the questions. If you miss out something or someone has further questions you can send follow-up information. That is less time consuming than producing something different for every reader. Remember that delay means lost money and lost opportunity.

If your plan does not convince there is seldom any point going back with amendments.

> *A client had a two-page plan drawn up by a consultant and sent out to venture capitalists. Some months later we helped to rewrite it as a much fuller document but when this was sent to organisations which had received the previous version they said they had turned down the proposal and would not reopen it.*
>
> Corporate finance consultant

A bad first impression is very hard to shift.

29. Confidentiality

Confidentiality is often an important issue. There are ways of dealing with this:

- Get the recipient to sign a confidentiality agreement
- Insert a paragraph which binds the reader to secrecy
- Try to omit sensitive information (but the plan must have enough substance to be convincing).

Confidentiality
depending up
about confide
  The agreem

1. Defining tl
   that it is
   unauthori:

2. Binding the recipient of the information.

   (a) to keep it confidential

   (b) not to make use of the information in their busi-
       ness

   (c) only to pass the information to their staff and
       advisers and to bind them in the same way as they
       have agreed with you.

Some agreements will bind the recipient not to approach
your customers, suppliers or staff. They may be bound not
to enter your market, but such undertakings usually have
a time limit on them. The courts will not enforce an unreasonable constraint. Agreements frequently require the
recipient either not to make or to return any copies of the
plan at the end of discussions. I have never understood
how this can be enforced.

  Where the confidentiality undertaking is part of the plan
itself it comes at the front and states that, by accepting the
document, the recipient agrees to be bound by the undertaking.

  It is worth noting that legal action to enforce confidentiality undertakings is rare and, because of the cost, a bigger
proportionate burden to the smaller business.

Appendix:
Business Plan Contents – A Checklist

Not everything on this checklist needs to be in a plan for every business, but you may wish be sure there is a good reason for their omission.

You may want to reorder or use different headings. It is important that the relevant information is there and the story flows logically, not that you follow the checklist to the letter.

Front page
Title, Date document was produced, Contacts for further information, Confidentiality undertaking (Ch. 29), Disclaimer of liability (Ch. 8)

Summary (Ch. 1)
Index
Introduction
Background to proposal (Ch. 2)
History of organisation (*or previous relevant businesses*)
Outline of the business or organisation (Ch. 3)
The product/service: what it is; what it does; why it's special (*unique selling proposition*)
The market (Ch. 4)
Size . . . growth . . . trends, Customers, Competitors, Sourcing, Manufacturing processes, Sales and distribution, Premises and plant
Trading summary (Ch. 5)
Past trading (if any), Forecasts, Assumptions, Seasonality, Turnover; gross profit; overheads; profit before interest and tax, Balance sheet, Cash flow forecast: monthly cash position

Management (Ch. 2)

Background of key managers, Organisation structure: staffing levels and skills

The proposal (Ch. 6)

Amount to be raised (*amount contributed by you*), How it is to be used and when, Existing bankers/financiers, Security you are offering (if any)

Strategy (Ch. 13)

Where your business is going, How you will get it there, Why you are different

Risk (Ch. 7)

Areas of risk . . . what happens if? . . . break-even

Appendices (Ch. 25)

Illustration and support for the plan